Rejoice! A Child Is Born

Reflections on Birth and Growth

Herb & Mary Montgomery

Winston Press

Acknowledgments

Material has been quoted from the following books:
How to Raise a Human Being by Lee Salk and Rita Kramer, Random House
Child Sense by William E. Homan, M.D., Basic Books, Inc.
What Do You Say to a Child When You Meet a Flower? by David P. O'Neill, Abbey Press
Baby and Child Care by Dr. Benjamin Spock, Hawthorn Books, Inc.
The Sense of Wonder by Rachel Carson, Harper & Row
Guiding Your Child to a More Creative Life by Fredelle Maynard, Doubleday & Co., Inc.
The Psychology of Children's Art by Rhoda Kellogg with Scott O'Dell, CRM, Inc.
How to Survive Parenthood by Eda J. LeShan, Random House
Children the Challenge by Rudolph Dreikurs and Vicki Soltz, Hawthorn Books, Inc.
A Parent's Guide to Children's Reading by Nancy Larrick, Doubleday & Co., Inc.
The Power of Play by Frank and Theresa Caplan, Doubleday & Co., Inc.
Your Child Is a Person by Stella Chess, M.D., Alexander Thomas, M.D., Herbert G. Birch, M.D., Viking Press
Escape from Childhood by John Holt, E.P. Dutton & Co., Inc.
A Child to Change Your Life by Thomas D. Murray, Alan Bailey Press
The Prophet, by Kahlil Gibran, Alfred A. Knopf

Photographs are from the following sources: John Arms—41; Camerique—5, 13, 14, 16, 32; Rohn Engh—34, 63; Stuart Klipper—46; Jean-Claude Lejeune—39, 43; Herb Montgomery—18, 26, 36; Robert Maust—Cover; Holly Maxson—61; Florence Sharp—8, 44, 48; Strix Pix—21, 50, 56, 58, 64; Bob Taylor—10, 22, 53, 54; Vivienne—6, 24, 29, 31.

Copyright © 1977 by Herb & Mary Montgomery
Library of Congress Catalog Number: 77-78259
ISBN: 0-03-022966-9
Printed in the United States of America

Winston Press, 430 Oak Grove, Minneapolis, Minnesota 55403

5   4   3   2

Contents

The Beginning

Few things touch us so profoundly as the birth of a child. The first exciting days inspire us to become the very best of parents. *Rejoice! A Child Is Born* celebrates this feeling and the relationship we hope to build with the child during infancy and the early years.

The birth of a daughter or son raises many questions. What will this child of ours become? How will we get along? What kind of parents will we be? The answers come only with time. They come little by little as we form a family and grow into our role as parents.

Love is where parenting begins, and it needs to be given freely, unconditionally. At first we may think we could never feel anything but warmth and tenderness for this baby who is so much a part of ourselves. But to be forever loving is not easy. Sometimes we have unloving thoughts. Many mothers and fathers experience moments — or even extended periods — when they have doubts and regrets about their parenthood. At such times we need to be reminded that although raising a child has its difficulties, it also offers rewards. To discover them, we have only to look beyond frustrations and open ourselves to the satisfaction of guiding a small and helpless child toward becoming a caring and independent adult.

Rejoice! A Child Is Born includes a number of quotations that we personally found helpful as we passed through the early years with our own children. The rest of the book is something of a love letter from a parent to a child. It's a hope-filled sharing of moods, feelings, and dreams that accompany parenthood.

From our experiences we've gleaned two guidelines for the early years. The first is to believe in ourselves. The second is to believe that *we* can grow, as well as our child.

Believing in ourselves enables us to sort through the things we hear and read about raising children and then decide what is suitable for our family. But what happens if we follow a course of action and find it's not working out? That's when guideline number two — believing we have the ability to grow — comes in.

Knowing that we can grow right along with our child allows us to make mistakes. Even though we sometimes fail, that doesn't mean we are failures. Learning from mistakes and starting over again is what growth is mainly about.

We sincerely hope that your family's journey is a joy-filled one and that our book will be a gentle reminder to look with wonder at what both you and your child are becoming. Rejoice, we say, for a child is born!

Mary and Herb Montgomery

One: Let there be touching...
for it makes a child feel at home in the world

The waiting is ended, my child, and you are born at last. How different that makes me feel — close to you and yet somehow a stranger. Let us not be strangers for long. Let us quickly begin to learn from one another.

What an abrupt change birth is! From the warmth and protection of the womb you have come into this foreign place with its bright lights and frightening sounds. Here the air can chill as well as warm your tiny body. Newborn stranger, I am your friend, your protector. I am here to love and care for you.

The rhythms of holding and feeding you and lulling you to sleep build my confidence. I yearn for all to be well between us. I want you to grow in trust and come to know the world as a beautiful and friendly place.

Can you sense what I am feeling? Does my touch already speak to you in some small measure of my dreams? Or do I seem a bit frightened and uncertain when I tend to your needs? You seem to take pleasure from the warmth and comfort of me, but we're not yet quite adjusted to each other. I am learning about you just as you are learning about me. And in these first days I want the gentleness of my touch to say, "You are in a safe place. Trust me to protect and care for you."

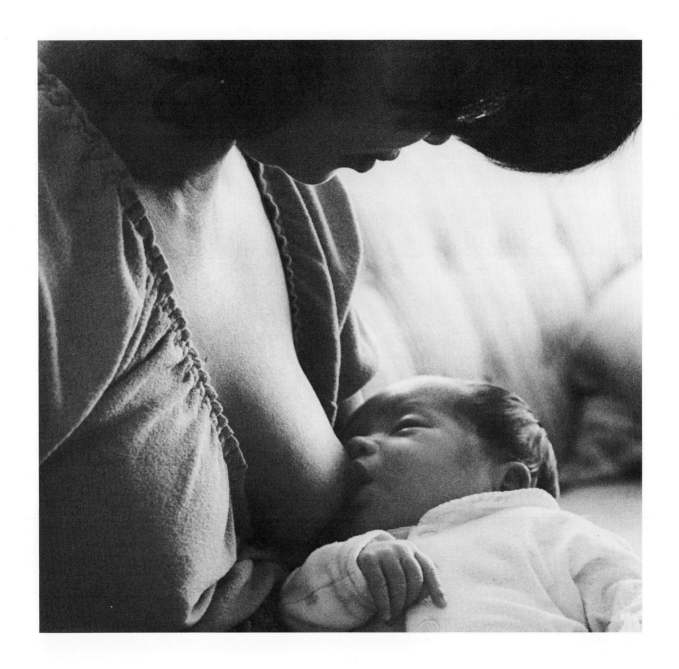

This is the important thing for babies to learn in the first months of life—that the world beyond the boundaries of their own bodies is a caring one, that there is someone who responds to their need to be free of discomforting tensions and that it's worthwhile reaching out to others.

Lee Salk and Rita Kramer, *How to Raise a Human Being*

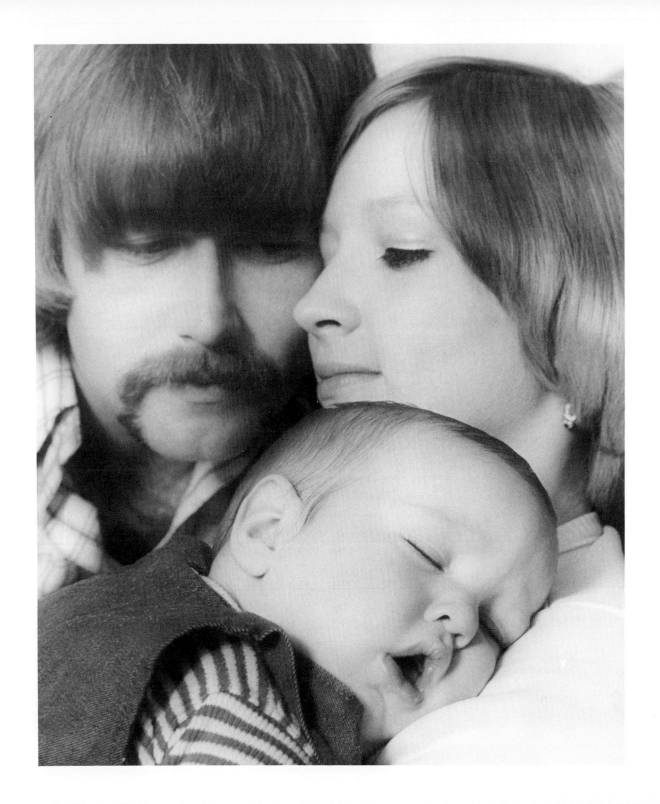

Two: Let there be love…
for what we receive we are able to give

As we live together day by day, I am discovering new meaning in the words "I love you." To love is to care at least as much for the welfare of another person as I care for myself. It is an unselfish action which begins within me and moves outward, giving life its fullest meaning.

Because I love you, it doesn't matter whether you are fretful or peaceful, plain or beautiful, chubby or thin. I accept you as you are. In doing so, I find that love leads me to seek what is best for you and for us as a family.

I give you my supportive love, trusting that you are going to have the strength and will to grow. In time, you will have your own contribution to make, and I hope you, too, choose to become a giving person.

My *words* of affection have no meaning for you yet. So for now I share love through the tone of my voice, the touch of my hand, and the expression on my face. Of course there are moments when I am not at my best. You will discover that though I smile, I also frown; though I speak softly, my voice can also be harsh; though I have patience, I am also impatient.

Take the best of me and my affection. My love for you is a gift I pass on with the confidence that you in turn will one day be able to love.

The type of love most important for the normal personality development of the child is the kind that says, "I love you...not for what you do or don't do, but just because you're you."

. . .

This is the kind of love that builds self-confidence, creates a good self-image, leads to a willingness to try without fear of the consequences of failing.

William E. Homan, M.D., *Child Sense*

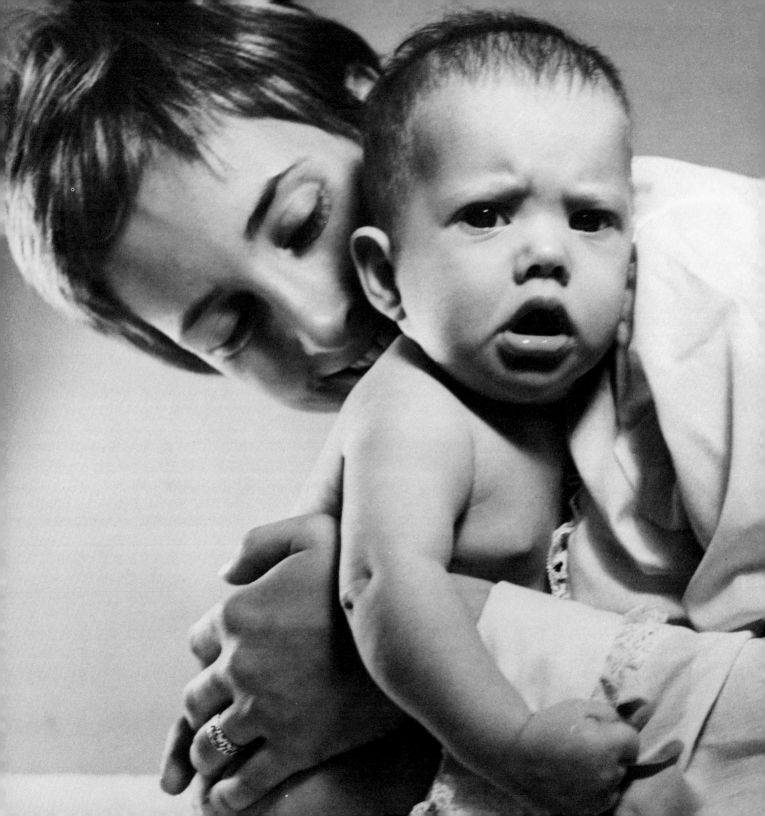

Three: Let there be feelings...
for they are natural responses

When your sudden cry alerts me to a desire which you cannot yet express in any other way, I come to you. Day or night I come to help if I can.

Are you hungry? Wet? In pain? Feeling a need for human contact? How perplexed I am by your crying when I cannot interpret it! Then I wish you could speak. How much simpler it would be if you could tell me in words what you need or where you hurt!

There is a part of you I cannot now understand and there is a part of me you cannot now understand. So already we have secrets from each other. Some of them we will reveal through our years of life together.

What you can't yet know is that confusion comes with parenthood. I love you, but your many demands can also make me resentful, irritated, angry. All these negative feelings are within me. Sometimes they erupt—just like your cries—and when they do, I feel guilty. It's as though I've betrayed myself and the love I think I should feel for you all the time.

People can spend a lifetime trying to become honest about their feelings. I'd like to get off to a good start and be open right from the beginning. Feelings are real and they're natural. When they're troubling us, we need to get help from understanding friends or counselors. We need to reach out to others, just the way you now call out to me.

Parents, enjoy your children
        be in joy with them
        look into their eyes
        be with them
        be for them.
Be relaxed with your children
        be unworried
        be carefree
        have fun.
Don't be afraid
        of loving them too much
        of making mistakes with them
        of being wrong
        of apologizing.
Then your children
        will love you
        and you will love them
        and love covers up our faults.

David P. O'Neill, *What Do You Say to a Child When You Meet a Flower?*

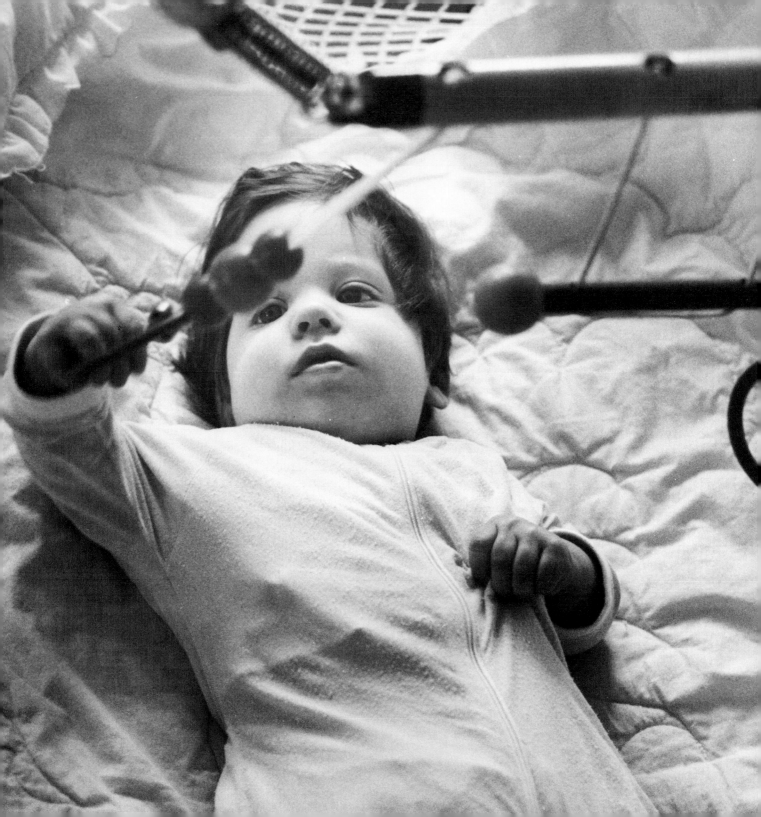

Four: Let there be play...
for it is the work of childhood

Watching you, I realize why so many of us grown-ups enjoy playing with babies. You free us of the restrictions we've become so accustomed to. With you I'm free to wrinkle up my face and invent new words. This kind of play puts me in touch with what is gentle and good about myself.

As I reflect, I see again what a difference there is between being childlike and childish. To be like a child is to be open, lovable, playful. How good that is! I want to encourage the child within myself.

Tiny as you are, it's hard to visualize you running and joining in games with other children. I'm sure that day will come, but now you play alone, using only your eyes. Movement in the room and light at the window catch your attention. I watch as you gaze with a kind of fascinated wonder at the swaying of the mobile over the crib.

It is a milestone day when you become aware of your hands and play with them as though they're the most wonderful of toys. What pleasure there is in experiencing the bend and feel of fingers! What a delight for you to find that hands can grasp and pull! Play, I can already see, is much more than something you do to amuse yourself.

While playing, you develop skills and make discoveries that help you understand your surroundings. I encourage your quest to make sense of all there is to see and touch, because I'm beginning to understand that play is both the fun and work of childhood.

The baby passing a rattle from one hand to the other or learning to crawl downstairs, the small boy pushing a block along a crack in the floor, pretending it's a train, are hard at work learning about the world. They are training themselves for useful work later....

Dr. Benjamin Spock, *Baby and Child Care*

Five: Let there be exploration...
for it is the path to discovery

Explorers have the courage that leads them around dark corners. Explorers believe they can climb a little higher and fulfill dreams. You were born an explorer. This makes you both a delight and an irritation! I'm eager for you to grow and develop your abilities, but explorers also face dangers. As you creep and crawl, I feel the need to protect you from the bumps and frustrations that lie all around.

Still, I urge you on from crawling to walking. I applaud your first successful steps, even though they are sure to take you further into the inviting land of No-No! There are drawers I don't want you to open, steps to stay away from, a vase that's not for touching.

How shall we get along now that this new dimension is added to our relationship? My putting away dangerous or delicate things allows you more freedom and makes this place where we live a home for you as well as for grown-ups. We'll have more rules now, but I'll try to make them reasonable.

Quickly you discover there's much you can explore by yourself, and that adds to your independence. It's possible to retrieve the stuffed animal you threw under a chair or find your way to me in another room. How many discoveries you've made in such a short time! Keep that urge to go exploring. It's a lifelong path to discovery that will help you satisfy curiosity and reach out to dreams.

Exploring nature with your child is largely a matter of becoming receptive to what lies all around you. It is learning again to use your eyes, ears, nostrils and finger tips, opening up the disused channels of sensory impression.

Rachel Carson, *The Sense of Wonder*

Six: Let there be wonder…
for it nourishes the spirit

What delight you take in ordinary things! Shadows on the floor or a pail full of water absorb your interest. You live in a world of constant surprise and find pleasures all around you. You have a sense of wonder that I'll do my best to keep alive.

On a walk with me, you spy a twig which seems as marvelous as any manufactured toy. You pick it up, taste it, wave it, carry it along. Then you come upon another treasure which holds your attention until your curiosity has been satisfied.

You are fascinated by raindrops on the window as well as a parade of ants on the sidewalk. I have known this sense of wonder myself while watching the night-sky stars. How sad that delight in the ordinary gets dulled by the events of everyday living! Speeding through the world of things, we grown-ups trade off the magic of rainbows for a shiny car we can touch. We forget how to kick off our shoes and walk barefoot in the grass.

All the wonder-makers of my past are still available to me. And you, my child, have the strength to pull me back to the wonder days. When we're together, I slow my pace a bit and allow my senses to come alive. It's so nice to know that ordinary things can still delight me. The gift of wonder makes the setting of the sun and the smile of a friend special experiences that nourish my spirit. I hope that you, too, will keep this gift alive within yourself.

All healthy children begin with an enormous interest in the world about them, a freshness and luminosity of vision. A four-year-old, marveling at the blurred ribbons of color in a grease puddle, bends closer: "It's a dead rainbow!" A five-year-old whose foot has fallen asleep wriggles in amazement: "My toes feel like ginger ale!" A three-year-old studies the night sky as if it were the first sky ever and announces solemnly, "Well, I see night is navy blue."

Fredelle Maynard, *Guiding Your Child to a More Creative Life*

Seven: Let there be creativity...
for it expresses individuality

Are you as creative as I like to believe? While exploring the paper with your crayon, you seem to sense a design all your own. What an ability to concentrate! I find myself wondering if you have a special talent in art.

Most of us are more creative than we realize. We create whenever we use our minds to rearrange ideas or materials. The poet who rearranges old words to write a new poem is being creative. So is the cook who blends leftovers with herbs to prepare a tasty soup. Creativity won't necessarily lead to financial gain, but it will result in a rich and satisfying expression of our individuality.

I look for ways for you to express yourself. I give you sand to shape and empty boxes to build with. Though it leads to noisy music, I give you a spoon and a pan and let you reinvent the drum. I provide paints and a place where you can work without your spills upsetting anyone.

Probably you won't have the artistic talent of a Picasso or the musical talent of a Beverly Sills, but the only way for you to know is to follow the creative path wherever your skills lead. Like every parent I look at you through the eyes of hope. If your talent is a rare gift, I'll be especially pleased. But if your talent is more ordinary, I'll still love and accept you just the way you are.

It is not hard to appreciate the art of early childhood. It is only necessary to know that there is in children's art no intent to create a picture in the adult sense of the word. To find a crooked house, on a crooked street, should not cause alarm. The house stands askew, inviting the rain, just as a matter of simple design.

Rhoda Kellogg with Scott O'Dell, *The Psychology of Children's Art*

Eight: Let there be questions…
for they are doors to understanding

Sometimes you ask questions simply to get my attention. I do that myself when I feel lonely. At other times you come to me for information to satisfy your curiosity, and I'm not always sure how to answer. What a challenge you are when you wonder, "Why is the sky blue?" "Who is God?" "What makes the kitty purr?"

Your questions give me the feeling that there's a door between us. I can choose—with my answer—to keep the door closed or to open it. When I say, "I'm busy" or "We'll talk about that later," I'm refusing to open the door. How easy it is to shut you out of my life without meaning to! If my answer is harsh or my words are angry, it's as if I've slammed the door in your face. I don't want that to happen, because it's sure to discourage you.

When you ask a question, that's the time you're the most ready to learn. Even when I'm rushed I can give you my attention for a moment. Maybe I can't satisfy you completely, but I can give you a brief and friendly reply. Then the door will be open, inviting future questions.

People have laughed at some of my questions. Oh, how that hurts! Laughter is never a good answer. Whenever I can, I'll do my best to tell you what you want to know and help you make sense out of the world that's yours to grow into.

Knowledge about child development can help us become more self-confident, flexible, resilient and resourceful, *but it cannot produce perfect children.*

. . .

Every normal, healthy child is upsetting, unlovable and difficult at times.

Eda J. LeShan, *How to Survive Parenthood*

Nine: Let there be praise...
for it inspires growth

You call me to come and look at the tower of blocks you've built. It stands precariously balanced, and when I express my delight, your grin tells me how much you need praise and approval. They mean a lot to me, too. When I've done something well, I like to have other people tell me so. Knowing I'm successful in one venture encourages me to try another.

I see you having successes like buttoning your coat or learning to pedal a tricycle. These may appear slight to us grown-ups, but they are big for you. My words of praise seem to call forth the best in you and help you believe in yourself. That's very important because you will probably achieve whatever you think you can.

Believing in yourself will free you to get on with what you want to do instead of holding back and wondering if you're good enough to try.

At first your feelings of success will be formed by the reactions of others. In time you will learn to decide individually when your accomplishments are truly worthwhile. Like a skilled musician who knows people sometimes applaud even a weak performance, you will have your own sense of value.

Give your best to whatever you do. Then, even when you receive no praise, you will still have both dignity and pride. You will be successful in your own eyes just as you are now successful in mine.

Encouragement is more important than any other aspect of child-raising. It is so important that the lack of it can be considered the basic cause for misbehavior. A misbehaving child is a discouraged child. Each child needs continuing encouragement just as a plant needs water.

Rudolph Dreikurs and Vicki Soltz, *Children the Challenge*

Ten: Let there be security...
for it leads to self-confidence

I always feel warm and proud when I walk hand in hand with you. My hand provides security and you usually stay close beside me. But lately I've noticed a change. Although you still grasp my fingers when we are in unfamiliar places, you're quicker to let go. We've reached the point where you're less in need of the security of me.

What mixed feelings I have! Of course I want you to become independent, but I enjoy being needed and feeling important. Be patient as I learn to let go little by little. I still want to protect you from the potential hurts and frustrations of which I'm so aware.

Becoming self-confident involves you in both advancing toward the unknown and retreating to the known. Home is what you know best, and if you are to grow in inner security, it needs to be a safe place from which you can proceed at your own pace. I hope life in our home is helping you understand that you are loved even when you're being unlovable. Take from that a sense of belonging and the confidence to move on into your own life.

I trust you'll discover that walking alone is always easier when we've begun with the good experience of walking together. And for those times when you need security, my hand is always there. All you need do is reach for it.

Few activities create a warmer relationship between child and grown-up than reading aloud.

Nancy Larrick, *A Parent's Guide to Children's Reading*

Eleven: Let there be imagination...
for it expands the mind

What is happening in your imagination? Are you playing? Running away? Trying to make sense of experiences?

At times I eavesdrop on your imaginative play to learn about myself as well as you. When you're playing parent to a doll and your voice suddenly fills with harsh discipline, I'm aware that you are being me. I've given you a model that I'd like to improve a bit! Then, just as quickly, you're comforting that doll. How wise you are, playing out both the worst and best of me. I go my way, feeling good about how you're developing.

Imagination allows you to shed feelings of being small and helpless. In imagination you work with all your experiences and interpret both what is and what might be.

While pretending to be a fire fighter going off to battle a blaze, you bring together all the brave behavior you've seen and heard and make it your own.

Sometimes I'm concerned about your imaginary friend who seems so important. But you willingly leave that pretend friend when a real child knocks at our door. In just a little while the two of you are together creating still another world of make-believe.

Balance the imaginary with the real, but keep your imagination growing through use. Besides giving pleasure, it will help you apply old ideas in new ways and let you turn problems upside down to discover new solutions. With a little nurturing, your imagination will serve you well for a lifetime.

Children need a long period of make-believe play to strengthen their spontaneity and self-expression. They need at least four years to build an "as if" world of their own and to pretend freely and revel in their fantasy and dreams.

Frank and Theresa Caplan, *The Power of Play*

Twelve: Let there be friends...
for they share our lives

Sharing doesn't come naturally. Early in your childhood you are content to play alone. Blocks and dolls are fun. Piles of sand and dirt attract you. Even when you are with another child, you act as if no one else is really there. Each of you plays alone and talks alone.

But there comes a day when you discover that certain kinds of play require another person. It's more fun to run when there's someone to race with you and tumble laughing to the grass. And how can you play store if there's no one to be a customer?

I'll do my best to put you in touch with others close to your age, but then it will be up to you to decide if they'll become your friends.

You'll have to work at learning to get along. It's a lifetime task. In the beginning I help by teaching you to take turns and not throw sand at others. I'll try to end playtime before it leads to fights and tears, but gradually more and more of the give-and-take of play with others is up to you. Playmates who become special people are more than someone to play beside. They are people with whom to share your ideas and feelings. Treat them as you like to be treated and you'll discover the secret of being a friend.

Children behave differently in their play because they *are* different. Some are more gregarious than others. Some are noisier and more active; others are more imaginative or more interested in doing things....

Stella Chess, M.D., Alexander Thomas, M.D., Herbert G. Birch, M.D., *Your Child Is a Person*

Thirteen: Let there be quiet time...
for it invites harmony

You rush toward me, upset and complaining that all the fault is in others. I hurt with you and want to comfort you. How do I best explain that it is not only the other who is to blame? You, too, have gotten out of tune and out of touch with yourself.

For the moment your unhappiness overwhelms you. Unlike some of us adults who are slow to admit our need, you run in search of an immediate comforter to lift your spirit so that you may sing life again.

I put my arms around you and let you cry. That may be all you need when life is chaotic—another person who will lovingly accept your tears. At other troubling moments you may need quiet time, a nap, or a calming walk with me.

When the harmony of my own life is disrupted, I need time alone to rediscover what is good and true about myself and my experiences. Quiet reflection restores my perspective and enables me to think clearly once again.

I've often reestablished an inner peace with myself while holding and rocking you. At other times I've renewed my spirit by driving, writing to a friend, walking, praying. Getting back in touch with myself gives me a sense of what's important. Best of all, it helps me reach out to you with healing love whenever you need it.

Children are not particularly happy or carefree; they have as many worries and fears as many adults, often the same ones. What makes them seem happy is their energy and curiosity, their involvement with life; they do not waste much time in brooding.

John Holt, *Escape from Childhood*

Fourteen: Let there be joy...
for it frees the heart

When you were born, I knew joy—an experience even richer than happiness, richer than delight! I was filled with fresh appreciation of life and all the possibilities that come with it. Rejoice! I told myself, for a child is born. A new person has come to share the freedom and the flowers and the heartbreak and the hope with those of us who already know them.

Joy is freely available to all of us. To make it ours we need only take time: time to listen to nature and one another and time to celebrate both the peaks and the valleys of life. Joy then is with us like a gentle breeze on a warm day, refreshing our spirit and reminding us of our blessings.

Good friends and good weather and good times call forth joy, but it can also be present in the midst of turmoil and anxiety. When we least expect it, we realize that sadness is not forever and that present troubles will pass. Then joy rises within us and we see a bright spot in the darkness, a cause for hope even in despair.

Through sharing and celebrating life with you, I hope to guide you toward an appreciation of joy. It is very much like love. Both help us understand at a deeper level what it means to be alive.

I'll tell my children that the happiness of human beings is too often measured in unrealistic lengths of time. I want them to realize that life is not lived in lifetimes or even seasons, but in sunny mornings and snowy afternoons, in picnics in the yard....

Thomas D. Murray, *A Child to Change Your Life*

Fifteen: Let there be trust...
for it expresses our faith in each other

Days of your babyhood slip ever so gently into my memory. When I look at you now, I see only hints of the infant you used to be. In a certain light I still see a shadow of the you I cuddled in my arms and coaxed to walk. How can it seem so long ago and yet as yesterday?

Have we gotten off to the right start? I want only the best for you. I hope that you'll go beyond me in some way. Surely that is a dream shared by all generations of parents.

You and I still have many years together, but much of the person you will grow up to be has already been shaped. From now on one of the things with which you and I will be concerned is freedom.

We'll struggle to decide how much is enough. Giving you ever greater freedom and responsibility has not always been easy for me. I've wanted so many times to protect you and do myself what for you was difficult or frustrating. Still, the two of us have grown, sometimes slowly and sometimes in spurts. I now know that what I'm trying to do is not protect you from the future but prepare you for it.

Since birth you have put your trust in me. Now I must trust more and more in you. I trust you to keep on growing as a very special person. As your parent, I put my faith in you, believing that the world is a little better simply because you are here.

You may give them your love but not your thoughts,
For they have their own thoughts.
You may house their bodies but not their souls,
For their souls dwell in the house of tomorrow,
        which you cannot visit, not even in your dreams.
You may strive to be like them, but seek not to make
        them like you.
For life goes not backward nor tarries with yesterday.
You are the bows from which your children as living
        arrows are sent forth....

Kahlil Gibran, *The Prophet*